Decorated Cupcakes

Frances McNaughton

This edition published in 2012
By **SpiceBox**™
12171 Horseshoe Way
Richmond, BC
Canada V7A 4V4

First published in 2012
Copyright © SpiceBox™ 2012
Text and photographs copyright © Search Press Limited 2009

ISBN 10: 1-77132-028-1
ISBN 13: 978-1-77132-028-3

CEO and Publisher: Ben Lotfi
Author: Frances McNaughton
Editorial: Cynthia Nugent
Creative Director: Garett Chan
Art Director: Christine Covert
Design & Layout: Charmaine Muzyka
Production: James Badger, Mell D'Clute
Sourcing: Janny Lam
Photography: Roddy Paine Photographic Studios

For more SpiceBox products and information, visit our website:
www.spicebox.ca

Manufactured in China

1 3 5 7 9 10 8 6 4 2

Contents

Introduction

Small is the new big! Cupcakes are a very popular way of celebrating any special occasion. They can be a colorful and tasty display for any party table. Some modern weddings even choose cupcakes as the centerpiece. Even if you don't have a special occasion, why not just make cakes for family and friends? It's a great way of practicing recipes and icing ideas to use on larger cakes.

There are many different cake recipes which can be used to make delicious cupcakes – in fact, most cake recipes for large cakes are also suitable for making small cakes.

More and more people are discovering the delights of cake decorating by giving cupcakes a whirl. I hope you have fun trying some of my ideas, and that these projects will spark a few ideas of your own.

Making Cupcakes

Ingredients:

- 1/2 cup (125 ml) butter, softened
- 1 cup (250 ml) sugar
- 2 eggs
- 1 tsp (5 ml) vanilla
- 2 cups (500 ml) flour
- 2 tsp (10 ml) baking powder
- 1/2 tsp (2 ml) salt
- 1/2 cup (125 ml) milk

1. Preheat the oven to 350°F (175°C). Line a 12-cup muffin pan with paper baking cups.

2. In a large bowl, cream together butter and sugar. Beat in eggs one at a time. Beat mixture until very creamy. Stir in vanilla and milk, mix well.

3. In a second bowl, whisk together flour, baking powder, and salt. Using an electric mixer, gradually blend the dry ingredients into the liquid mixture. Beat for 2 minutes.

4. Spoon mixture into paper baking cups. Bake for 18–25 minutes until golden brown, and cake springs back when lightly pressed with your finger. Allow to cool for a few minutes and then transfer to a wire rack. Cool fully before icing.

If you'd prefer not to bake, a large range of plain or iced cupcakes and muffins are available in supermarkets and bakeries for those who just want to do the decorating! Candies, melted chocolate, chocolate-covered finger cookies, golden sugar, edible glitter flakes, and fudge have been used in this book to create simple designs.

Alternative Flavors

Chocolate: add 4 tablespoon (60 ml) cocoa to the dry ingredients.

Lemon: add 1 teaspoon (5 ml) grated lemon rind, and 1 tablespoon (15 ml) lemon juice to liquid ingredients.

Coffee: add 2 teaspoons (10 ml) instant coffee.

You can make different sizes of cupcakes by using mini- through to muffin-size paper baking cups. Depending on the design you want to make, the cake can be baked so that it only fills up to the top of the baking cups, for a flat design; or it can be baked with more cake in the baking cups, to form a dome when it is baked. If the cake rises more than you want, or is cracked on the surface, simply slice the top to make it domed or flat.

Basic Tools

- Piping bags with decorating tips
- Small cutters in flower, petal, leaf and heart shapes
- Round biscuit cutters (plain and frilly)
- Quilt embosser
- Cutting wheel
- Flower center tool
- Small palette knife
- Small rolling pin
- Small, sharp scissors

Over the Rainbow

Materials: (decorating materials and tools are available from craft stores and some grocers)
• cupcakes in brightly-colored baking cups

Icing:
• ½ cup (125 ml) vegetable shortening
• 2 ½ cups (625 ml) icing sugar
• 1 tsp (5 ml) vanilla
• 2–3 tbsp (30–45 ml) cream or milk
• food colourings: blue, red, yellow and green

Tools:
• small palette knife
• at least four parchment-paper piping bags
• plain decorating tips (or snip the end off a paper piping bag)

Colorful rainbow cupcakes like these will brighten any party table.

Instructions:

1. Make the icing by mixing the shortening, sugar, and vanilla, then beat in cream a tablespoon at a time to form a smooth, soft icing for piping. Using vegetable shortening keeps the icing white for the clouds, and blue for the sky. If you prefer to use butter for a better flavor, the clouds will look creamy and the blue will not be as bright.

2. Mix a portion of the icing with red food coloring, another with yellow and another with green. Fill the piping bags (with or without the piping tubes) with a large spoonful each of white, red, yellow, and green icings.

3. Mix blue coloring into the rest of the icing and spread over the surface of each cake with a palette knife.

4. Pipe a curved red line halfway around each cake, then repeat with the yellow, then the green.

5. Pipe little white clouds at the ends of the rainbow.

Life's a Beach

Materials: (decorating materials and tools are available from craft stores and some grocers)
- cupcakes in brightly-colored paper baking cups
- fondant icing mix
- gum paste and pink gum-paste color (fondant and gum paste are available from craft stores and some supermarkets)
- food coloring: blue and pink
- golden sugar

Tools:
- small palette knife
- Use the outlines (right) to make a template for the flip-flops
- sharp knife or cutting wheel
- small rolling pin
- bowl

For a variation, add a few drops of liquid green color to desiccated coconut or granulated sugar to look like grass. Dip half of the cup cake in the 'grass' to stick it on. Perfect for a summer party.

Instructions:

1. Color the gum paste pink. Roll out and cut out the soles of the flip-flops using your flip-flop templates. Cut out thin straps, dampen them with water and stick them on.

2. Mix the fondant icing, following the instructions on the packet. Gently warm to body temperature in a bowl over hot water, stirring occasionally. The fondant will be quite runny, but sets quickly as it cools.

3. Color half of the fondant blue, and leave the other half white.

4. Spread blue fondant on half of each cake, and white on the other half.

5. Sprinkle the white half with golden sugar to look like sand.

6. Lay the flip-flops on top of each cake. If you want to make sure they are stuck on, spread a small dot of warmed fondant or buttercream under each heel to act as glue.

Halloween Pumpkin

Materials: (decorating materials and tools are available from craft stores and some grocers)
- cupcakes baked in scary paper baking cups

Buttercream Icing
- 1/2 cup (125 ml) butter
- 2 1/2 cups (625 ml) icing sugar
- 1 tsp (5 ml) vanilla
- 2–3 tbsp (30–45 ml) cream
- food coloring: orange and green
- dark chocolate, melted

Tools:
- small palette knife
- parchment-paper piping bags
- small and medium-sized plain decorating tips (or snip the end off a parchment-paper piping bag)

Make as many different scary pumpkin faces as you like for a Halloween party, or to hand out to trick or treaters.

Instructions:

1. Make the icing by mixing the butter, sugar, and vanilla, then beat in cream a tablespoon at a time to form a smooth, soft icing for piping.

2. Mix green coloring into a small portion of the icing and orange into the rest. Fill a small piping bag fitted with the small decorating tip with a small spoonful of green icing. Fill a larger piping bag fitted with the medium tip with orange-colored icing.

3. Start piping with a straight orange line down the centre, and then pipe either side, increasing the curve as each line is piped.

4. Pipe a few green lines at the top for leaves.

5. Put a small amount of melted dark chocolate into a small piping bag, and snip off a tiny piece of the end. You can then pipe a face directly on the cake. Alternatively, pipe it on to parchment paper, leave to set, peel off and stick onto cupcakes.

Halloween Ghost

Materials: (decorating materials and tools are available from craft stores and some grocers)
• cupcakes baked in spooky baking cups

Icing
• 1/2 cup (125 ml) white vegetable shortening
• 2 1/2 cups (625 ml) icing sugar
• 1 tsp (5 ml) vanilla
• 2–3 tbsp (30–45 ml) cream or lemon juice
• 24 marshmallows
• black piping gel

Tools:
• small palette knife
• parchment-paper piping bag
• medium-sized plain decorating tips (or snip the end off a parchment-paper piping bag)

These cute cupcakes can be made with any type of cake flavor. Choose your favorite packaged cake mix to make these up in a jiffy.

Instructions:

1. Ice cupcakes

2. Place a large marshmallow on top to make the ghost.

3. Cut a marshmallow into smaller pieces for arms. The stickiness of the cut marshmallow may be enough to attach it, but if not, glue marshallows together with icing.

4. Use piping gel to make eyes and mouth, and swirl a little bit of white frosting onto the top using a piping bag.

Beautiful Basket

Materials:
- cupcakes
- fondant icing mix
- gum paste and yellow gum-paste coloring for the primroses
- icing (see recipe on page 9). Add up to 2 tablespoons (30 ml) cocoa until you get the shade you like.

Tools:
- small palette knife
- parchment paper piping bags
- piping tube: small basketweave, rope or star
- small primrose flower cutter
- ball tool
- small rolling pin

Add colorful jelly beans or tiny Easter eggs to make this an Easter basket.

Instructions:

1. Spread the fondant icing on top of each cake. This can be colored if you prefer.

2. Fill a piping bag fitted with a basketweave, rope, or star decorating tip with chocolate icing.

3. Start by piping the handle on top of each cake.

4. Then pipe a basket: start at one side, piping a vertical line, then pipe short lines across it, leaving the width of the piping tube between each line. Pipe a second vertical line, just covering the ends of the short horizontal lines. Pipe short lines across this second line, filling the gaps between the first and second vertical line. Pipe a third vertical line and continue piping short horizontal lines across. Continue across the cake until the basket is complete.

5. Roll out gum paste that you've tinted yellow and cut out primrose flowers. Stick onto cupcake at the top of the basket by pushing through the center with the ball tool.

Fluffy Duck

Materials: (decorating materials and tools are available from craft stores and some grocers)
- cupcakes baked in baking cups that coordinate with the design
- fondant icing colored with blue food coloring
- gum paste tinted red or orange
- icing (see page 9) tinted yellow
- small amount of melted dark chocolate for the eye
- food coloring: yellow

Tools:
- small palette knife
- piping bags
- large plain decorating tip

Make a swan with white icing (page 9), beginning with long, curved head and neck. Do beak and eye with piped chocolate.

Instructions:

1. Spread the warmed blue fondant on each cake.

2. Drop the decorating tip into the piping bag, and fill the bag with yellow icing.

3. Pipe a large ball for the head.

4. Pipe a large, fat curved teardrop for the body, starting at the front. Pipe a smaller teardrop for the wing, marking feathers with a palette knife.

5. Make a small beak from the colored gum paste and stick it into the soft buttercream.

6. Pipe an eye with melted dark chocolate.

Lionheart

Materials: (decorating materials and tools are available from craft stores and some grocers)
- cupcakes baked in gold foil baking cups
- buttercream icing (page 9) to which you've added:
- 2 tbsp (30 ml) cocoa
- gum paste and gum-paste yellow and brown coloring for the face. (you can substitute soft commercial fudge, warmed in the hands and shaped, for the the gum paste).
- small amount of melted dark chocolate for the features

Tools:
- piping bags
- decorating tips: basketweave, small rope or star
- small rolling pin
- heart cutter
- toothpick

To make the tiger, use a plain decorating tip and orange-colored buttercream (see page 9) to pipe onto the cake. Shape the face in the same way as the lion using white gum paste. Pipe stripes, eyes, nose, and eyebrows with melted dark chocolate.

Instructions:

1. Make buttercream icing as on page 9, blending the cocoa with the icing sugar before adding butter and cream. Fill a piping bag fitted with a basketweave, rope, or star piping tube with icing.

2. Pipe wiggly lines starting at the centre and finishing with the point over the edge of the cake.

3. Mold colored gum paste or soft fudge into a heart shape. Use the picture as a guide, or roll out the paste and cut out using a heartshaped cutter. Lay it on the cake.

4. Shape two small ovals for the cheeks. Press into place and mark with a toothpick.

5. Make two tiny balls of paste, flatten them slightly and pinch at the base for the ears.

6. Pipe melted dark chocolate to make the eyes, nose and eyebrows.

Baby Blanket

Materials: (decorating materials and tools are available from craft stores and some grocers)
- cupcakes baked in baby-themed baking cups
- gum paste and gum-paste colors to make skin, and blue or pink for the quilt
- icing sugar for rolling out gum paste
- small amount of jam or buttercream, to stick the blanket to the cake

Tools:
- small rolling pin
- quilting embosser (quilted look can also be done with a knife and ruler)
- tiny feet mould (alternatively, the feet can be modelled by hand from gum paste or piped using white frosting (page 9)
- cutting wheel or knife
- square template made from card, slightly larger than the top of the cake

These delicate cup cakes are ideal for a baby shower or christening, or as a gift to celebrate a new arrival.

Instructions:

1. Color the gum paste with blue or pink, sprinkle work surface with icing sugar to prevent sticking, roll out.

2. Emboss surface to look like a quilt.

3. Using your template, cut out the icing.

4. Spread a small amount of buttercream or jam cake and lay the icing blanket on top. Overhang the corners

5. Color gum paste for skin color. Make tiny feet and stick on top of your cupcake.

Knitted Novelties

Materials:(decorating materials and tools are available from craft stores and some grocers)
- at least seven cupcakes in colored baking cups to match icing
- white icing (page 9)
- food coloring: yellow, green and blue are illustrated here, but choose your own colors
- candy sticks for the knitting needles
- small amount of white gum paste for heads of needles

Tools:
- piping bags
- plain small decorating tips

This colorful collection of cupcakes would be ideal for celebrating the birthday of a friend who loves knitting.

Instructions:

1. Divide the icing and mix in your chosen colors. Put each into a piping bag fitted with a decorating tip.

2. Pipe straight lines across each cake as shown, to look like loosely rolled balls of wool.

3. Pipe a spiral line down one of the candy sticks and push the end of the stick into one of the cupcakes.

4. Continue piping loops in rows along the stick to look like knitting.

5. Push the other candy stick into the same cupcake.

6. Dampen the top ends of the candy sticks and press a small flattened ball of sugarpaste on each one.

Spanish Fan

Materials: (decorating materials and tools are available from craft stores and some grocers)

- cupcakes baked in red baking cups
- buttercream icing (page 9)
- red food coloring
- color dust: red
- metallic dust: gold
- gum paste

Tools:

- small palette knife
- clean soft paint brushes
- piping bag
- decorating tip: star or rope

This fantastic cup cake has a Spanish look, but you could change the colors to create an oriental theme.

Instructions:

1. Make fans by rolling out gum paste and cutting in the shape of the template. Score lines on the fans with a palette knife.

2. Spread red buttercream on the cupcakes.

3. Pipe around the edge of each cake using a star or rope decorating tip.

4. Paint the fans with red dust and and edge with gold dust.

5. Carefully push the fans into the tops of the cupcakes.

Ice Cream Dream

Materials: (decorating materials and tools are available from craft stores and some grocers)

- flat-bottomed ice cream cones
- puffed rice cereal
- 3 1/2 oz (100 g) white chocolate, melted
- buttercream (see page 9)
- ice cream sauce, fruit flavor

Tools:

- piping bag
- decorating tip: large star or rope

These ice cream dreams are a departure from traditional cup cakes, with chocolate-covered crispy rice cake as the base. You could make your own fruit purée or melt chocolate to drizzle over the top, then sprinkle with tiny sweets or chopped nuts.

Instructions:

1. Mix melted white chocolate with the puffed rice cereal, coating each grain so they'll stick together. Fill each of the ice cream cones to a domed top (see photo detail). Leave to cool.

2. Pipe a large swirl of buttercream, starting from the outside edge and coming up to a point in the middle.

3. Drizzle the top with fruit flavor ice cream sauce.

Flower Pot

Materials: (decorating materials and tools are available from craft stores and some grocers)
- chocolate cup cakes, domed on top
- chocolate-covered cookie sticks or chocolate sticks
- small jelly candies
- white chocolate, melted

Tools:
- parchment paper

These potted cupcakes make a lovely gift alternative to a plant. They would also be a real hit at children's parties.

Instructions:

1. Spoon a small blob of melted white chocolate onto parchment paper. Lay the end of a chocolate-covered cookie stick or chocolate stick into the chocolate. Leave to cool and set (this can be speeded up by putting it in the refrigerator).

2. When set, spoon another small blob of chocolate on top of the first one, and stick on colored jelly candies to form a flower. Use melted chocolate to attach a couple of green jelly candies for leaves lower down the stick. Leave to cool and set.

3. Push the chocolate stick stem into the top of the cupcake.

Wedding Cake

Materials: (decorating materials and tools are available from craft stores and some grocers)
- cupcakes baked in silver foil cups, flat-topped
- mini-cupcakes baked in foil cups for chocolates
- fondant icing (page 11)
- gum paste
- small amount of buttercream (page 9)
- food coloring: green

Tools:
- small rolling pin
- small petal-shaped cutter
- piping bag with plain decorating tip
- palette knife

Made in different-colored paper liners, these beautiful cakes could also be served for wedding anniversary celebrations. Bake the cakes in gold foil liners, and use ivory-colored fondant.

Instructions:

1. To make an arum lily, thinly roll out gum paste. Cut out petals with the cutter. Roll each one between your fingers to form a spiral with the point of the petal at the top. Leave to one side to set.

2. Spread warmed white fondant icing over each cake, placing the tiny cake on top of the larger one straight away so that it will stick.

3. Pipe small green stems and long leaves on the cakes and press the flowers into place.

Ladybugs

Materials: (decorating materials and tools are available from craft stores and some grocers)

- cupcakes with domed tops (or carved to form a smooth dome)
- gum paste, colored, reserving some plain for the eyes
- gum-paste coloring: red, black,
- buttercream or jam for sticking the gum paste to the cake
- icing sugar for rolling out paste

Tools:

- small rolling pin
- palette knife
- small circle cutters

These happy insect cupcakes are going to bring a smile to any child's face. Or, serve them at a grown-up garden party for a whimsical touch.

Instructions:

1. Look in your kitchen for a circle template large enough to cover the whole of the dome of the cake. Use a bowl or saucer for the red circle template, and a drinking glass for the black ladybug face.

2. Spread a little buttercream or jam on each cup cake ready to stick on the gum paste.

3. Color and roll out the red gum paste, and cut out using your large template. Lay the paste on the cake and smooth out evenly. Mark a line across the middle for the wings using the palette knife.

4. Color and roll out the black gum paste, cut out with your smaller circle, dampen it slightly with water and stick it on the edge of the cake

for the face. Trim to the edge of the red paste.

5. Use the edge of a small circle cutter to press in a smiling mouth.

6. Eyes and spots on the back can be cut out using small circle cutters, or molded by hand. Make two small circles of un-colored gum paste and stick them on the face for eyes. Make two smaller black circles to place them on top of the white. Two larger circles of black stuck on the back will make the ladybug's spots.

Lavender

Materials: (decorating materials and tools are available from craft stores and some grocers)
- cupcakes baked in purple baking cups
- gum paste
- gum-paste coloring: purple
- yellow nonpareils
- candied lavender
- buttercream icing (page 9)
- 1 tsp (5 ml) lavender extract
- 2 drops purple food coloring
- icing sugar for rolling out paste

Tools:
- small rolling pin
- palette knife
- small flower cutter
- ball tool

Instructions:

1. Tint and flavor buttercream icing with lavender extract and purple food coloring.

2. Ice the cupcakes and place a sprig of candied lavender on top of each.

3. Roll out gum paste that you've tinted mauve and cut out flowers. Shape petals and set aside to dry. Ring each cupcake with lavender flowers by pushing through the center with the ball tool. Dab or pipe a dot of icing in the center of each flower and place a yellow nonpareil on top.

Lavender is a lovely flavor to mix with chocolate. Candied lavender may not be available outside of specialty shops but it is worth looking for because it's delicate appearance, beautiful color and distinct flavor captures the spirit of warm summer days perfectly for your next summer picnic!

Christmas Cupcakes

Materials: (decorating materials and tools are available from craft stores and some grocers)

• cupcakes baked in Christmas-themed baking cups
• gum paste
• gum-paste coloring: green
• nonpareils, red
• buttercream icing (page 9)
• icing sugar for rolling out paste

Tools:

• small rolling pin
• palette knife
• holly cutter

If you wish to bake the cupcakes from scratch, you can enhance the "Christmas-y" flavor by adding:

• 1/2 cups (125 ml) candied fruit, finely chopped
• 2/3 cup (170 ml) raisins,
• 1/4 cup (65 ml) pitted dates, finely chopped

to the basic cake recipe on page 6. The resulting cupcake will be similar to a light, moist Christmas cake. Yum!

Instructions:

1. Measure out nuts and fruit. Make cake batter following the recipe on page 6. Fold in nuts and fruit, Spoon batter into paper liners.

2. Dust work surface with icing sugar. Roll out gum paste that you've tinted green and cut out holly shapes. Set aside to dry.

3. Ice cupcakes with buttercream.

3. Stick holly leaves into buttercream and arrange groups of nonpareils at the base of the leaves.